"TEACH ME YOUR WAYS, O LORD,
THAT I MAY LIVE ACCORDING
TO YOUR TRUTH!"

Psalm 86:11

HOW TO USE THIS BOOK

1 Set aside time each day to discover...study... enjoy... learn... God's Word. You can study/write each verse in one day, or take several days to complete the "lesson."

First, look up the Scripture verse in your Bible.

READ *Romans 8:38*

QUICK TIPS Try to understand the <u>context</u> of the Scripture by reading a couple verses before and after the verse listed.

2 Trace the letters in the Bible verse.

TRACE

"Nothing can ever

separate us from

God's love."

3 Write the verse on your own.

WRITE

"Nothing can ever

QUICK TIPS If writing the entire verse is too difficult for your child, pick out a couple words for them to write instead.

HOW TO USE THIS BOOK

Use a dictionary, or bible concordance, to look up the definitions to the words listed. (Sometimes there will be a question to answer instead.)

WORDS

"Nothing can ever separate us from God's love."
Romans 8:38

Look up & write down the definitions to these words:

separate: *to part company;*
to keep apart or divide

love: *a feeling of personal*
attachment or deep affection

QUICK TIPS

All the Scripture in this book is from the New Living Translation (NLT). You don't have to use that version, but it will make it easier to find and define the words in the Bible passage.

Draw a picture to illustrate the verse.

QUICK TIPS

When you illustrate the verse, it helps you take the time to understand what the verse means and how it can apply to your life.

Matthew 19:14

"Let the children come to me. Don't stop them!"

WORDS

"Let the children come to me. Don't stop them!"

Matthew 19:14

Answer this question:

Read Matthew 19:13-15. Why did Jesus want the children to come to Him?

DRAW

Draw a picture to illustrate this verse.

Romans 8:38

"Nothing can ever
separate us from
God's love."

"Nothing can ever separate us from God's love."

Romans 8:38

Look up & write down the definitions to these words:

separate:

love:

Draw a picture to illustrate this verse.

Proverbs 3:5

"Trust in the Lord with all your heart."

WRITE

**WORDS**

"Trust in the Lord with all your heart." Proverbs 3:5

Look up & write down the definitions to these words:

trust:

heart:

DRAW

Draw a picture to illustrate this verse.

John 3:36

"Anyone who believes in God's Son has eternal life."

WRITE

"Anyone who believes in God's Son has eternal life."

John 3:36

Look up & write down the definitions to these words:

believe:

eternal:

Draw a picture to illustrate this verse.

TRACE

"Jesus told him, 'I am the way, the truth, and the life.'"

WRITE

WORDS

"Jesus told him, 'I am the way, the truth, and the life.'"
John 14:6

Look up & write down the definitions to these words:

way:

truth:

life:

DRAW

Draw a picture to illustrate this verse.

Psalm 23:1

"The Lord is my
shepherd; I have all
that I need."

"The Lord is my Shepherd; I have all that I need."

Psalm 23:1

Look up & write down the definitions to these words:

Shepherd:

need:

Draw a picture to illustrate this verse.

READ

TRACE

"... but God intended it all for good."

WRITE

WORDS

"...but God intended it all for good." Genesis 50:20

Look up & write down the definitions to these words:

intended:

good:

DRAW

Draw a picture to illustrate this verse.

Exodus 12:13

"When I see the blood,
I will pass over you."

"When I see the blood, I will pass over you." Exodus 12:13

Answer this question:

Read Exodus 12:11-13. Why was the blood on the doorpost so important?

Draw a picture to illustrate this verse.

Genesis 1:1

"In the beginning God
created the heavens
and the earth."

WORDS

"In the beginning God created the heavens and the earth." Genesis 1:1

Answer this question:

How did the world and everything in it begin?

DRAW

Draw a picture to illustrate this verse.

Psalm 118:24

"This is the day the
Lord has made. We
will rejoice and be
glad in it."

WRITE

"This is the day the Lord has made. We will rejoice and be glad in it." Psalm 118:24

Look up & write down the definitions to these words:

<u>rejoice:</u>

<u>glad:</u>

Draw a picture to illustrate this verse.

TRACE

"People judge by
outward appearance,
but the Lord looks at
the heart."

WRITE

 **WORDS**

"People judge by outward appearance, but the Lord looks at the heart." 1 Samuel 16:7

Answer this question:

What is the difference between how God judges people, and how we as humans judge each other?

 **DRAW**

Draw a picture to illustrate this verse.

Psalm 121:2

"My help comes from
the Lord, who made
heaven and earth!"

WRITE

WORDS

"My help comes from the Lord, who made heaven and earth! Psalm 121:2

Answer this question:

Why should you ask the Lord for help?

DRAW

Draw a picture to illustrate this verse.

Romans 8:11

"The Spirit of God,
who raised Jesus from
the dead, lives in you."

WORDS

"The Spirit of God, who raised Jesus from the dead, lives in you." Romans 8:11

Answer this question:

What's so amazing about the Holy Spirit living inside of you?

DRAW

Draw a picture to illustrate this verse.

Psalm 119:105

"Your word is a lamp
to guide my feet and
a light for my path."

"Your word is a lamp to guide my feet and a light for my path." Psalm 119:105

Look up & write down the definitions to these words:

guide:

light:

Draw a picture to illustrate this verse.

Romans 3:22

"We are made right
with God by placing our
faith in Jesus Christ."

WORDS

We are made right with God by placing our faith in Jesus Christ." Romans 3:22

Look up & write down the definitions to these words:

right:

faith:

DRAW

Draw a picture to illustrate this verse.

James 4:8

"Come close to God,
and God will come
close to you."

"Come close to God, and God will come close to you.
James 4:8

Answer this question:

How do you "come close" to God? (Read James 4:7-10)

Draw a picture to illustrate this verse.

Luke 19:10

"The Son of Man came
to seek and save
those who are lost."

"The Son of Man came to seek and save those who are lost." Luke 19:10

Look up & write down the definitions to these words:

seek:

save:

lost:

Draw a picture to illustrate this verse.

Psalm 86:5

"O Lord, you are so good, so ready to forgive."

WORDS

"O Lord, you are so good, so ready to forgive..."

Psalm 86:5

Look up & write down the definitions to these words:

<u>ready:</u>

<u>forgive:</u>

DRAW

Draw a picture to illustrate this verse.

Matthew 28:6

"He is risen from the
dead, just as he said
would happen."

WORDS

"He is risen from the dead, just as he said would happen." Matthew 28:6

Look up & write down the definitions to these words:

risen:

dead:

DRAW

Draw a picture to illustrate this verse.

READ

TRACE

"This is the message of Good News...that there is peace with God through Jesus Christ."

WRITE

 **WORDS**

"This is the message of Good News...--that there is peace with God through Jesus Christ...." Acts 10:36

Look up & write down the definitions to these words:

peace:

through:

 **DRAW**

Draw a picture to illustrate this verse.

READ

Revelation 4:8

TRACE

"Holy, holy, holy is the

Lord God, the

Almighty."

WRITE

Holy, holy, holy is the Lord God, the Almighty...."

Revelation 4:8

Look up & write down the definitions to these words:

holy:

almighty:

Draw a picture to illustrate this verse.

Matthew 1:23

"They will call him
Immanuel, which
means' God is with us.'"

WORDS

"...they will call him Immanuel, which means 'God is with us' " Matthew 1:23

Answer this question:

This verse is talking about Jesus. Why did God come to earth to be with us?

DRAW

Draw a picture to illustrate this verse.

Luke 8:50

"Don't be afraid. Just have faith."

 **WORDS**

"Don't be afraid. Just have faith...." Luke 8:50

Look up & write down the definitions to these words

faith:

 **DRAW**

Draw a picture to illustrate this verse.

"Don't be afraid. Just have faith...." Luke 8:50

TRACE

"Don't worry about anything; instead, pray about everything."

WRITE

"Don't worry about anything; instead, pray about everything." Philippians 4:6

Look up & write down the definitions to these words

worry:

pray:

Draw a picture to illustrate this verse.

Hebrews 13:16

"Don't forget to do good and to share with those in need."

"Don't forget to do good and to share with those in need."   Hebrews 13:16

Look up & write down the definitions to these words

<u>do good:</u>

<u>share:</u>

Draw a picture to illustrate this verse.

If you need tools to help your children grow in
their walk with the Lord, use this QR Code to go to

DIGGINGINTOGOD.COM

Made in the USA
Monee, IL
20 September 2024